LOOKING AT COUNTRIES

Looking at
ETHIOPIA

Kathleen Pohl

Reading consultant: Susan Nations, M.Ed.,
author/literacy coach/consultant in literacy development

Gareth Stevens
Publishing

Please visit our web site at www.garethstevens.com.
For a free color catalog describing Gareth Stevens Publishing's list
of high-quality books, call 1-800-542-2595 (USA) or 1-800-387-3178 (Canada).
Gareth Stevens Publishing's fax: 1-877-542-2596

Library of Congress Cataloging-in-Publication Data

Pohl, Kathleen.
  Looking at Ethiopia / Kathleen Pohl ; reading consultant, Susan Nations.
      p. cm. — (Looking at countries)
  Includes bibliographical references and index.
  ISBN-10: 0-8368-9062-0   ISBN-13: 978-0-8368-9062-4 (lib. bdg.)
  ISBN-10: 0-8368-9063-9   ISBN-13: 978-0-8368-9063-1 (softcover)
  1. Ethiopia—Juvenile literature. I. Title.
DT373.P635   2008
963—dc22   2008003120

This edition first published in 2009 by
Gareth Stevens Publishing
A Weekly Reader® Company
1 Reader's Digest Road
Pleasantville, NY 10570-7000 USA

Copyright © 2009 by Gareth Stevens, Inc.

Senior Managing Editor: Lisa M. Herrington
Senior Editor: Barbara Bakowski
Creative Director: Lisa Donovan
Designer: Tammy West
Photo Researcher: Charlene Pinckney

Photo credits: (t=top, b=bottom, l=left, r=right, c=center)
Cover © Robert Harding Picture Library Ltd./Alamy; title page © Tony Waltham/
Robert Harding World Imagery/Corbis; p. 4 Frances Linzee Gordon/Lonely Planet Images;
p. 6 © Franck Guiziou/Hemis/Corbis; p. 7t © Miglavs/Danita Delimont/Alamy; p. 7b
© Martin Harvey/Alamy; p. 8 Ariadne Van Zandbergen/Africa Imagery; p. 9t Boris Heger/
AP; p. 9b © Tony Waltham/Robert Harding World Imagery/Corbis; p. 10t © Trevor Smithers
ARPS/Alamy; p. 10b © Jon Arnold Images Ltd./Alamy; p. 11t © Gavin Hellier/JAI/Corbis; p. 11b
© Images of Africa Photobank/Alamy; pp. 12–13 © Sean Sprague/Alamy; p. 14 Chris Fairclough/
CFW Images; p. 15t © Friedrich Stark/Alamy; p. 15b © Robert Harding Picture Library Ltd./Alamy;
p. 16 Frances Linzee Gordon/Lonely Planet Images; p. 17t © Robert Preston/Alamy; p. 17b
© Andrew Holt/Alamy; p. 18 Chris Fairclough/CFW Images; p. 19t Jonathan Alpeyrie/Getty Images;
p. 19b © Viviane Moos/Corbis; p. 20l © Keith Levit/Alamy; p. 20r John Dominis/Time Life Pictures/
Getty Images; p. 21 Manoocher Deghati/IRIN; p. 22 © Wolfgang Kumm/dpa/Corbis; p. 23t
© Andy Chadwick/Alamy; p. 23b © Richard Human/Alamy; p. 24 © Borderlands/Alamy; p. 25t
© Puchinger/imagebroker/Alamy; p. 25b © David Gray/Reuters/Corbis; pp. 26–27 Shutterstock (3)

Printed in the United States of America

1 2 3 4 5 6 7 8 9 11 10 09 08

Contents

Words that appear in the glossary are printed in **boldface** type the first time they occur in the text.

Where Is Ethiopia?

Ethiopia is a country in northeastern Africa. It borders five other countries. Sudan is to the west. Somalia and Djibouti (juh-BOO-tee) are to the east. Kenya is to the south, and Eritrea is to the north.

Did you know?

Ethiopia and its neighbors make up the Horn of Africa. This area has a shape like the head and horn of a rhinoceros. Look at the map. Can you see the horn?

EUROPE

AFRICA

Indian Ocean

ETHIOPIA

Atlantic Ocean

Africa is four times as big as the United States. Ethiopia is almost twice as big as the state of Texas.

The kings who once ruled Ethiopia loved lions. This lion statue is in a plaza, or square, in the capital, Addis Ababa.

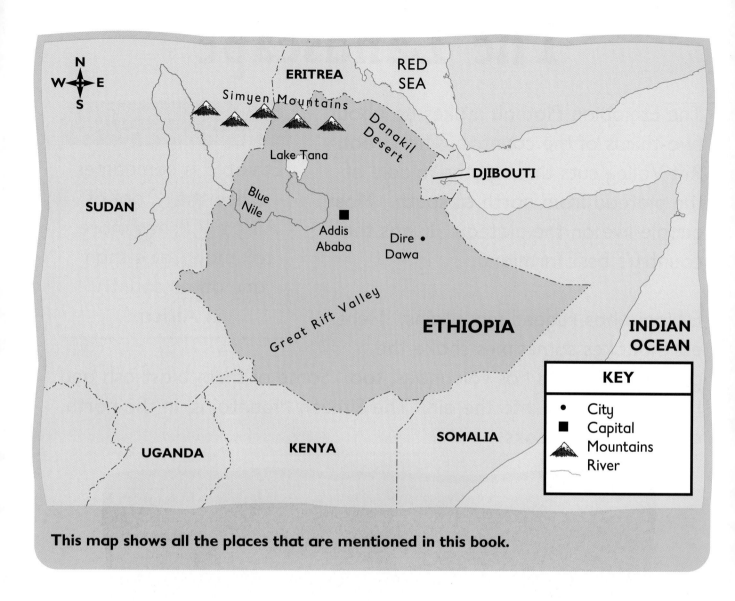

This map shows all the places that are mentioned in this book.

Ethiopia is close to both the Indian Ocean and the Red Sea. The country is **landlocked**, however. That means it has no coasts.

Addis Ababa is the capital. It is the center of government. The city sits on a **plateau**, or a high, flat area of land. It has a mix of tall, modern buildings and small grass huts. Some parts of Addis Ababa have paved streets. Other parts have dirt roads.

The Landscape

The Ethiopian Plateau makes up about two-thirds of the country. The Great Rift Valley cuts through the middle of the plateau from north to south. Most people live on the plateau. It has the country's best farmland.

Ethiopia has rugged mountains. Here, earthquakes sometimes shake the ground. Ethiopia has volcanoes, too. Some of them blast ash and hot, melted rock into the air. The Simyen Mountains, in the north, are the tallest peaks.

The Blue Nile Falls are an awesome sight! This waterfall is on the Blue Nile River.

Some termite nests are as tall as trees! Termites are insects that eat wood.

The gelada baboon is a rare animal. It lives only in Ethiopia.

The longest river in Ethiopia is the Blue Nile. It flows from Lake Tana, the country's biggest lake. The Blue Nile feeds into the Nile River. The Nile is the longest river in the world!

Around the central plateau are lowlands, with grassy plains, forests, and deserts. Animals such as rhinos, lions, and **jackals** roam in the wild. Colorful birds and flowers live there, too. Insects called termites build huge nests that look like piles or cones of dirt. Some nests are as tall as trees!

Weather and Seasons

Most of Ethiopia has a warm climate. The hottest and driest area is the Danakil Desert. This desert gets very little rain. The highlands, where the most rain falls, have cooler temperatures. The tops of some mountains have snow on them.

Salt beds crack in the heat of the sun in the Danakil Desert. People mine the salt and sell it.

Monsoons sometimes cause floods. Heavy rains can leave roads and bridges under water.

Parts of Ethiopia are covered with dry grasslands. Few trees grow there.

The country's rainy season lasts from June to September. People call that season the "big rains." Sometimes too much rain falls at one time. Winds called **monsoons** bring very heavy rains and sometimes cause floods.

In some years, no rain falls. During long dry times, crops die in the fields. People starve because of **famines**, or extreme food shortages.

Ethiopian People

More than 76 million people live in Ethiopia. It is one of the poorest countries on Earth. It is one of the oldest, too! Kings ruled at least part of Ethiopia for almost 2,000 years. Experts say the earliest humans lived millions of years ago in the area that is now Ethiopia.

The Karo people paint their faces. They live in the Omo Valley, in southern Ethiopia.

A priest stands in front of a church in Lalibela. The church was cut out of rock more than 800 years ago!

This girl has woven colorful bread baskets. She lives in the Ethiopian Highlands.

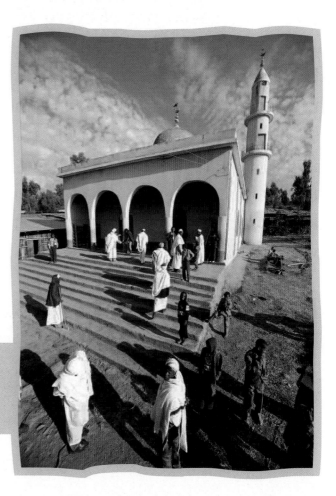

Muslims worship at this **mosque** in the Simyen Mountains.

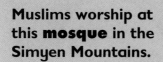

People from 80 different **ethnic groups** live in Ethiopia. The biggest groups are the Oromo and the Amhara. Each group of people has its own language and ways of life. Sometimes the groups fight each other. This type of fighting is known as **civil war**.

Most Ethiopians are Christian or Muslim. The main language of the country is Amharic. Many Ethiopians speak English, which is commonly taught in schools.

School and Family

Public school is free in Ethiopia. Only about six or seven out of every 10 children go to primary school, though. In the past, few girls were sent to school. The number of girls in school has doubled in the past few years.

Many schools are very poor. There is little money for books and teachers. One teacher may have as many as 70 students. Classes are sometimes held outdoors.

Two children study their lessons. In some places in Ethiopia, school is held outdoors.

In this classroom, students sit at desks to do their schoolwork.

Say cheese! This Ethiopian family is all smiles as they have their picture taken.

In the early grades, children study history, Amharic, English, and math. Many children have to leave school to work on family farms. Few finish more than six years of school.

Most families have several children. The father is usually the head of the house. Mothers mostly cook and care for the family. Women in Ethiopia do not have the same rights that women in some other countries have. Many girls marry when they are very young.

Country Life

Most Ethiopians live in the countryside. They live on small farms or in tiny villages. Most villages do not have lights or clean drinking water. Many people die from disease.

A lot of farmers are poor. They can barely feed their big families. A little, round grain called **teff** is the main food crop. Farmers also grow corn and wheat. In the southwest, many farmers grow coffee beans.

Some villages are just small groups of huts.

Ethiopian farmers use animals called **oxen** to pull wooden plows in the fields.

Most farmers in Ethiopia are too poor to own modern farm machines. They use oxen to pull plows.

Most homes in the countryside do not have running water. This woman gets water at a village pump.

Children help work in the fields. They chase birds away from the crops. They also look for firewood. Many children help care for goats, sheep, and chickens.

In the desert, people called **nomads** move from place to place. They look for good areas to find food and to herd their animals.

City Life

In Ethiopia, about one of every five people lives in a city. In recent years, more people have moved to the cities to look for work. Many houses there have electricity and running water. Cities also have more schools and better health care.

People wait for a train at the station in Addis Ababa. Most Ethiopians do not own cars.

Blue-and-white van taxis are familiar sights in the city.

These women shop at an outdoor market in Addis Ababa. The market is the largest in Africa.

Addis Ababa is Ethiopia's biggest city. It is home to more than 2 million people. This busy city has office buildings, banks, and shops. It is known for its large outdoor market.

The second-largest city is Dire Dawa (dee-ray DOW-ah). It is a major trade center.

Most people in the cities do not own cars. Many people walk to work. Others ride motorbikes or take buses or taxis.

Ethiopian Houses

In the country, many houses are made of dried mud, straw, and sticks. They have **thatched** roofs, which are made of grass or straw. Most houses are round, with only one room. In the north, some people live in stone houses.

Nomads take their houses with them as they move from place to place. Camels carry the tents made of animal skins.

Did you know?

Some Ethiopians bring their goats and sheep into their huts at night! This keeps the **livestock** (farm animals) safe from wild animals that might eat them.

Most huts are round and have thatched roofs. The roofs slant to help the rain run off.

In the city, some rich people live in big houses. Some people live in tall apartment buildings, too. Poor people live in grass huts or tin shacks. Their homes have no water or lights.

Some people in Ethiopia are **refugees**. They left other countries to escape danger, such as war. They live in huts or tents in crowded camps.

Refugees are people who have fled their homes. They live in tents in refugee camps.

In big cities, some people live in tall apartment buildings. Poor people live in small huts or shacks.

Ethiopian Food

Most people in Ethiopia grow the food they eat. They cook over a fire and eat one or two hot meals a day. The main food is **injera**, a kind of flatbread made from teff. It is cooked like a big pancake. People snack on this food. They eat it with spicy stews made of

A woman cooks injera over a fire. The flatbread looks like a giant pancake!

A typical breakfast may include wat and injera. Wat is a stew made of chick peas.

In the cities, people buy fresh fruits and vegetables at outdoor markets.

meat and beans, too. Families usually eat from one big dish in the center of the group.

Many Ethiopians also make bread from the root of the **ensete** (en-SEE-tee). That is a kind of banana plant. People eat boiled barley and roasted corn, too. They also grow potatoes, cabbage, beans, and mangoes. Some people raise sheep, goats, and camels for meat.

Many Ethiopians drink tej, a wine made from honey. They also drink coffee, tea, and a thin, sour milk called yogurt.

At Work

Most people in Ethiopia work on farms. Coffee beans grow on huge farms called **plantations**. The government owns the plantations. Coffee is the main **cash crop**. (A cash crop is grown to be sold, not used by farmers.) Other farm products include sugarcane, livestock, and beeswax.

In the cities, some women work outside the home. The workers in this factory sort coffee beans by hand.

A telephone worker hooks up wires and cables.

This nurse works at a health clinic.

Some people work in **factories** in cities. Factory workers make cloth, cement, leather, and shoes. Ethiopia trades goods with other countries, including the United States.

In cities, many people work in shops, restaurants, banks, or offices. Some are doctors or nurses. Others work for the government. A few people fish or work in the country's gold mines.

Having Fun

Most people in Ethiopia do not have much time for fun. Still, some Ethiopians enjoy playing sports. They like soccer and **ganna**, a kind of field hockey. People play basketball, volleyball, and tennis in cities that have courts. Some ethnic groups have their own sports. Stick fighting is a popular sport in southwestern Ethiopia.

Girls have fun playing a game of soccer after school.

Every year, people celebrate Timkat. The three-day festival is the most important religious holiday in Ethiopia.

Did you know?

Some of the best long-distance runners in the world have come from Ethiopia. Both men and women have won Olympic medals.

Grown-ups like to play chess, cards, and a board game called **gabata**. Children enjoy listening to folktales. They play games that are a lot like hopscotch and hide-and-seek.

Most holidays in Ethiopia are religious. People go to special church services. They also enjoy feasts, parades, and music.

This runner won a gold medal at the 2004 Olympic Games in Athens, Greece. His name is Kenenisa Bekele.

Ethiopia: The Facts

• The official name of Ethiopia is the Federal Democratic Republic of Ethiopia. It became a **federal republic** in 1994. It was once called Abyssinia (a-bah-SI-nee-ah).

• The president is the **chief of state**, or formal representative of the country. The prime minister is the head of the government.

• Ethiopians who are 18 years old or older may vote.

• Ethiopia is not often at peace. Sometimes its people are at war with one another. At times, Ethiopia is at war with its neighbors, including Sudan and Somalia.

• Eritrea used to be part of Ethiopia. Eritrea gained its independence from Ethiopia in 1993.

The flag of Ethiopia has three bars of green, yellow, and red. At the center is a blue circle with a five-pointed star.

Ethiopia's unit of money is the **birr**.

Lions with black manes are also called Abyssinian lions. Only male lions have black manes.

Did you know?

The lion is the symbol of Ethiopia. The country is famous for its lions with black manes. Many of them once roamed in Ethiopia. Today only about 1,000 of the lions live in the wild.

Glossary

ancestor — family member who lived in the past

birr — the unit of money in Ethiopia

cash crop — a crop, such as coffee, that is sold for money

chief of state — the formal representative of a country

civil war — a war in which people in the same country fight each other

ensete — a plant that belongs to the banana family. Ethiopians use the roots to make flour for bread.

ethnic groups — groups of people with the same cultures, traditions, and ways of life

factories — buildings where workers make goods

famines — great shortages of food

federal republic — a system in which the national government and the states have separate powers. Elected officials represent the people.

gabata — an Ethiopian board game

ganna — a game played in Ethiopia that is similar to field hockey

injera — the main food of Ethiopia, a flatbread made from teff

jackals — wild dogs with large ears, long legs, and bushy tails

landlocked — not bordered by water on any side

livestock — farm animals such as cows, goats, and sheep

monsoons — seasonal winds that bring heavy rains

mosque — a Muslim place of prayer and worship

nomads — people who move from place to place, living in tents and grazing their animals

oxen — the full-grown males of domestic cattle, usually used to pull loads on farms. Oxen are slow-moving but very strong.

plantations — large farms on which crops such as cotton, tobacco, sugarcane, and coffee are grown

plateau — a high, flat area of land

refugees — people who flee their country, often for political or religious reasons

teff — a tiny, round grain used to make flour for bread

thatched — made of bundles of grass, palm leaves, or straw

Find Out More

Fact Monster: Ethiopia
www.factmonster.com/ipka/A0107505.html

National Geographic People and Places: Ethiopia
www3.nationalgeographic.com/places/countries/
country_ethiopia.html

**United Nations CyberSchoolBus – Country
at a Glance: Ethiopia**
cyberschoolbus.un.org/infonation/index.asp?id=231

Publisher's note to educators and parents: Our editors have carefully reviewed these Web sites to ensure that they are suitable for children. Many Web sites change frequently, however, and we cannot guarantee that a site's future contents will continue to meet our high standards of quality and educational value. Be advised that children should be closely supervised whenever they access the Internet.

My Map of Ethiopia

Photocopy or trace the map on page 31. Then write in the names of the countries, bodies of water, cities and villages, land areas, and mountains listed below. (Look at the map on page 5 if you need help.)

After you have written in the names of all the places, find some crayons and color the map!

Countries
Djibouti
Eritrea
Ethiopia
Kenya
Somalia
Sudan
Uganda

Bodies of Water
Blue Nile
Indian Ocean
Lake Tana
Red Sea

Cities and Villages
Addis Ababa
Dire Dawa

Land Areas and Mountains
Danakil Desert
Great Rift Valley
Simyen Mountains

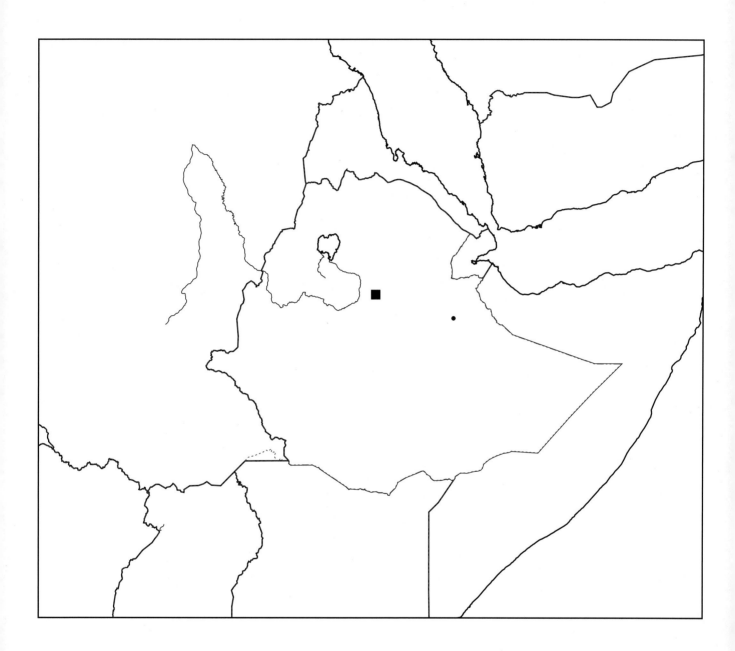

Index